INVASION

OF WALES

BY THE

SPIRIT

THROUGH
EVAN
ROBERTS

JAMES A. STEWART

REVIVAL LITERATURE

Tel: 1-800-252-8896
PO BOX 6068
ASHEVILLE, NC 28816
ISBN 1-56632-067-4

Printed in the United States of America

CONTENTS

Affectionately dedicated
to the memory of
REV. AND MRS. SYDNEY EVANS
whose labors for the Lord in Wales and India were so won-
derfully blessed. They now see the King in His beauty.

INTRODUCTION

Does it seem strange that a Scotsman writes about the great revival in Wales? If so, then may I explain that the reading and hearing of this mighty movement stirred me to my deepest depths when I was a young babe in Christ.

I first visited Wales in 1936 to speak at the Every Creature Missionary and Bible Conference in Swansea with Dr. Paul Rader, Dr. R. E. Neighbour, and Mrs. Charles E. Cowman. Many times since then I have had the privilege of speaking at this same convention, held in the grounds of the Bible College of Wales. Besides this, I ministered one year at the Llandridod Wells Convention (The Welsh Keswick). On each occasion I took the opportunity of living over once again these glorious days, not only with those who were saved during this time, but also with some of the leaders.

Mr. Evan Roberts' family have been so gracious to me down the years when I had occasion to visit them. What precious times I have spent at Island House, the birth place of the revivalist, and also the setting for those extraordinary months of communion with His heavenly Father. Here these friends very kindly drew aside the veil of intimate family life and let me into many of the secrets of these glorious times. Naturally, many of these incidents are too intimate and sacred to be placed in a book.

In all fairness to my fellow evangelists all over the world, I feel it necessary to state to the reader the difference between a spontaneous work of God in revival and a planned and prepared evangelistic campaign. If the Holy Spirit is not working in a mighty way in the churches before the evangelist comes, then it is necessary to have a well-organized preparation. Many evangelists have been sorely disappointed, not only in the poor spiritual preparation, but also in the lack of organized preparation for their evangelistic campaigns. Slipshod preparations are an insult to God. However, this book deals with spontaneous revival.

For my own personal views on the difference between preparation for Revival and for an Evangelistic Campaign, the reader may study two important books: *Evangelism Without Apology* (lectures given at Bob Jones University), and *Opened Windows*.

The greatest preparation of all is by prayer which results in confession of sin and mighty anointings of the Holy Spirit. No matter how great may be the crowd or the organization, if the Christians are not broken and burdened for souls and the Holy Spirit is not working, all is in vain.

James A. Stewart
Denmark, 1963

Chapter 1

WHEN THE SPIRIT CAME

Evan Roberts was not the author of the Welsh Revival. The Author of the Welsh Revival was none other than the Holy Spirit of God, Himself. Although Evan Roberts became the popular figure in the movement before the press and the public in November, 1904, it is well to note that the Great Awakening in Wales had its beginnings two years before this time in many parts of the Principality. And when the river of God was at full spate in the latter part of the year 1904 it was found that the Spirit was using for His instruments at least a hundred pastors, evangelists, and so-called "lay-people" for His work. While the Spirit's workings in revival spread into almost every nook and corner of the country, the ministry of Evan Roberts was in the main confined to one of its twelve counties. The fire of God burned in towns and villages which he did not visit. And in many of the places which he did visit, he found the fire was already there. His visit only fanned the flame.

One of the features of a true movement of the Holy Spirit in revival is that He does not depend on one human personality in His workings. As much as I love and admire Evan Roberts as a man of God, and as much as I appreciate how greatly his ministry was blessed in the movement in Wales, I must state that the whole lesson of this textbook on revival will have been missed if it leads the readers to glorify man instead of God.

It is true that there must be the human side of revival; "The sword of the Lord — and Gideon." It is true that God searches out and uses broken, clean vessels for His work, and that in Evan Roberts He found such a vessel. Moreover, during these years

He prepared and used hundreds of such instruments in different parts of the Principality who led thousands to Christ. These young converts, in turn, went out to witness to the grace and power of God. Yet, every one of these men and women would point the reader to the divine Spirit of God Who was the instigator and promoter of the mighty movement in Wales and surrounding districts in 1904-05.

Another outstanding feature of true revival is that the movement does not depend on money, organization, or advertising. You cannot organize or control the fire of God.

The astounding feature of this awakening was the lack of commercialism. There were no hymn books, no song leaders, no committees, no choirs, no great preachers, no offerings, no organization.

I have scanned newspapers of Wales which came out in 1904 and 1905 and found no paid advertisements there announcing the meetings. So far as I can discover in my research while reading magazines and books and asking numbers of people who were saved at that time, not one single dollar was spent in advertising the revivalists. As the late Lord Pontypridd once remarked, "The revival finances and advertises itself. There are no bills, no hired halls, no salaries."

The only time I can discover that a committee organized a planned evangelistic campaign for Evan Roberts was in the city of Liverpool in 1905. Even on this occasion the Spirit of God disrupted the plans and broke through the machinery by the time the revivalist arrived.

The movement was entirely under the control of the Spirit of God. Evan Roberts seems to have learned his lesson in the matter of making his own plans early in the revival. Just a few weeks before the revival broke out in his home church in Loughor, Evan had planned campaigns throughout Wales with his brother Dan and his friend Sydney Evans. Soon he was to discover that the Spirit had another plan — something better and deeper. After this, he greatly feared man's planning and organization. In my long talks with Sydney Evans and Mary Roberts-Evans, his wife, and also with the widow of Dan Roberts, I discovered that Evan would not announce any meetings for a week ahead. He simply announced a day or two ahead, if at all, that he hoped to be in a certain place at a given time. Even then it was not sure when, where, or if he would preach! He moved only with the Spirit. When the campaign was organized in Liverpool, the committee pressed him to state a definite time when he would come and begin meetings, but he refused to say and when he did eventually go there (his only meetings outside his beloved Wales) he gave the committee only a three or four days' warning. Even then, though 100,000 Welsh people in the great English city were longing and waiting to hear him, he insisted that he could not know in which of the crowded chapels he would speak at a given time!

Dan Roberts and Sydney Evans reaped a mighty harvest, but, like Evan, they simply obeyed the Spirit and went to districts where He told them to go. These were young men, just turned twenty and entirely unknown to the public, and they knew that apart from the presence and power of the Holy Spirit and His guiding hand, they would accomplish nothing. And when they arrived in a place, sometimes they preached and sometimes they did not. Sometimes they kept silent during the whole proceedings which would last for four or five hours.

It was for God that the people came to the meetings. In many cases they crowded chapels to overflowing, not even knowing whether the evangelist would be there or not. *Sometimes Evan Roberts would enter a meeting and sit on the front seat and say nothing for three hours.* Then he would stand up, preach and pray for some ten or fifteen minutes and sit down. The people, themselves, carried on under the influence of the divine Spirit.

While it is true that there were soloists and duets and special singers during these days such as Sam Jenkins, Misses S. A. Jones, Annie M. Rees, Anne Davies and others, these were never announced to sing. And when they did sing it was under the compulsion of the Spirit. The evangelist never called upon them to sing nor announced that they would sing. Sometimes they sang and sometimes they did not, according to the promptings of the Spirit. Sometimes these young ladies, instead of singing, would break out in fervent prayer and exultation. Often when they did rise to sing they would not be able to finish the song because they were so overcome by the power of God.

Another characteristic of true revival is that the Lord Jesus Christ, Himself, is the center of the attraction: —"It was noised that He was in the house." If the evangelist or the evangelistic party is the center of the attraction, then the work is of the flesh and not of God.

Nobody was more conscious of this fact than the popular revivalist, himself. He dreaded publicity. He dreaded newspaper reporters. He dreaded adulation. Many times he withdrew himself from the meetings when he felt that the people were coming to see and hear him only. In meetings where he feared he was the center of attraction he pleaded with agonized spirit that the people would look away to Christ and Him alone, or else the Holy Spirit would withdraw Himself from the movement. At other times he purposely refrained from speaking in the meetings because he sensed that the people came to see and hear *him* about whom they had heard rather than Jesus Christ Who had the blessing for them. Though he became by far the most publicized preacher in the world at that time, he repeatedly refused interviews with newspaper men who came from every part of the globe. He refused to be photographed except by members of his own family. He knew this awakening was of God and not from himself and that if people idolized him the Shekinah Glory would be withdrawn. Thus it was that when letters reached him from many different publishing firms throughout the world asking that they might write about him, he felt the Spirit would have him answer none of these, fearing that he would be robbing God of the glory due to His holy name alone. *Sometimes the revivalist sat among the people, praying silently, and then left without saying a word.* Visitors from different parts of the world were astonished to sit in crowded gatherings where people sang, prayed, and testified without the young prophet even being there to take part. The saintly F. B. Meyer, a matured Christian leader, upon watching him in the meetings, explained, "He will not go in front of the divine Spirit, but is willing to stand aside and remain in the background unless he is perfectly sure that the Spirit of God is moving him." Then he added, "It is a profound lesson for us all!"

So evident was it that the movement was a divine work that outstanding British Christian leaders came and stood in awe and bowed in adoration to God. Although famous preachers such as Gypsy Rodney Smith, F. B. Meyer, G. Campbell Morgan, General Booth, and many others visited the scene of blessing, in the majority of cases they only prayed or said a few words. Sometimes they sat quietly in the meetings while young people, and even children prayed, sang, and testified in the Spirit. These great men of God recognized the fact that this was not a revival come through great preachers nor through great preaching, but that it was a supernatural work altogether apart from either. They felt that their very personalities would hinder the meetings. *And why should great Christian leaders preach sermons when here before them they saw their sermons fulfilled!* Here was the answer to the agony of their prayers for the blessing upon the church of God and the salvation of lost souls. And besides — they could not have taken part unless the Holy Spirit had invited them to do so!

Chapter 2

THE DRIFT OF THE SPIRIT

The Holy Spirit, when He comes in power upon a church, a town, or a country, comes with His own strategy and His own order of working. Such is easy to follow in the Welsh Revival.

It was a revival for young people. Evan Roberts, himself, was only twenty-six years of age. Mary, his sister who took such an active part, was sixteen, while their brother Dan and her future husband Sydney Evans were around twenty. The "Singing Sisters," as they were lovingly called, were between the ages of eighteen and twenty-two. Thousands of young people, when they became converted, went everywhere testifying. Little children had their own prayer and praise meetings. The chapels were crowded out with the young.

It was a revival of singing. The Welsh are famous for their native gift of congregational singing. No part in the harmony of a tune is missing and most of the singers sing as those who have been thoroughly trained. Imagine, then, if you can, an instrument with its every string swept by the breath of the Spirit of God! As blessed R. B. Jones, a leader in the revival, said, "The fact is, unless heard, it is unimaginable and when heard indescribable. There was no hymnbook. No one gave out a hymn. Just anybody started the singing, and very rarely did it happen that the hymn started (no one knew by whom) was out of harmony with the mood at the moment. Once started, as if moved by a simultaneous impulse, the hymn was caught up by the whole congregation almost as if what was about to be sung had been announced and all were responding to the baton of a visible human leader. I have seen nothing like it. You felt that the thousand or fifteen hundred persons before you had become merged into one myriad-headed, but simple-souled personality. Such was the perfect blending of the mood and purpose that it bore eloquent testimony to a unity created only by the Spirit of God."

"The praying and singing," to quote another witness, "were both wonderful. No need for an organ. The assembly was its own organ as a thousand sorrowing or rejoicing hearts found expression in the Psalmody of their native hills."

It was a revival of prayer. Prayer mingled largely with praise. And what wonderful praying! It was praying that rent the heavens; praying that received direct answers there and then. The spirit of intercession was so mightily poured out that the whole congregation would take part simultaneously for hours! Strangers were startled to hear the young and unlettered pray with such unction and intelligence as they were swept up to the Throne of Grace by the Spirit of God. Worship and adoration was unbounded. Praise mingled with petitions as answered prayer was demonstrated before their very eyes, when their unsaved loved ones came into the meetings and were saved! What a contrast to our prayer meetings today!

It was a revival of soul-winning. Instead of a few preachers and a few of their church members testifying to the saving grace of the Lord Jesus, it seemed now as if every Christian in Wales had a burning agony for lost men and women. It was a most natural thing for a true believer to testify of his glorious Redeemer in the coal mine, in the tramcar, in the office and in the school. Thousands were saved through the personal witness of ordinary, common believers who spoke to them of the claims of Christ during ordinary conversation.

It was a revival of personal experience. How John and Charles Wesley would have revelled in these meetings! No wonder General William Booth was thrilled to hear the testimonies. It was worth traveling thousands of miles, even from Australia and New

Zealand just to be in one revival service, even though Evan or Dan Roberts or Sydney Evans was not there — just to hear the dynamic testimonies of the spiritual experiences of the Christians in Wales! Here was really the old-fashioned Methodist class-meeting over again — revived by the Spirit of God. Here was an intimate walk with God — a God with whom they had personal dealings and whom they had come to know in a deep, intimate way. Here was a God who answered prayer!

No wonder the people could not sleep and could not stay away from the meetings. No wonder the services carried on till two and three o'clock in the morning and then resulted in a march through the streets with the people singing the praises of the Lamb!

Many at the time and since then have criticized the emotionalism displayed in the meetings. Yes, when thousands of people are convicted of their sins and are gloriously saved by the grace of God, how can they contain their joy? When believers are elevated to a new, heavenly position in Christ and at the same time see the answer to years of agonizing prayer in the salvation of their loved ones, surely there must be shouts of joy and songs of adoration. The mountains had melted in God's presence and the heavens were opened. The Church in Wales had a new and glorious sight of their wonderful Lord. This was expressed in the following chorus which was called "The Love-song of the Revival":

> Wondrous Love, unbounded mercy!
> Vast as oceans in their flood:
> Jesus, Prince of life, is dying —
> Life for us is in His blood!
> Oh! what heart can e'er forget Him?
> Who can cease His praise to sing?
> Wondrous Love! Forever cherished,
> While the Heavens with music ring.

Chapter 3

O LORD, REND THE HEAVENS!

Every outpouring of the Spirit is preceded by earnest, agonizing, intercession, accompanied by a heart-brokenness and humiliation before God. This is followed by a recognition and honoring of the blessed Spirit. Pastors and flock alike in their churches are deeply concerned about the terrible discrepancy between the heart-stirring record in the Book of Acts and the present-day condition of the church. So it was in the little Principality of Wales before the month of November, 1904.

It is an impossible task to trace the beginnings of the awakening, either in individual hearts or in individual churches. One reason, no doubt, is that those who had the deepest experiences with their Lord were loath to reveal them publicly. These experiences were too sacred for them to divulge to the public. Many, I am sure, could have come forward and given personal and private witness to the first stirring in their own breasts, helping us trace the glorious beginnings of the revival, but somehow a veil of secrecy has been spread over these early days.

Suffice it to say that no revival is of sudden origin. When the revival manifests itself in a mighty way it comes suddenly as in the days of Hezekiah, but even so, its origins begin with the Holy Spirit of God moving effectively in individual lives in private. Let no one pray for revival — let no one pray for a mighty baptism of power who is not prepared for deep heart-searchings and confession of sin in his personal life. Revival, in its beginnings, is a most humiliating experience. When one, like Isaiah, sees himself in the light of God's holiness he must inevitably cry, "Woe is me!"

Deep spiritual awakenings, whether in local churches or in

whole countries, begin with desperate people like Hannah. God only answers prayers of desperate Christians — Christians who are tired and weary of cold, mechanical "services" before God; Christians who are heartbroken over the deadness of the professing churches and over sinners going to an endless hell; Christians who are desperate about their own spiritual condition. While it is true that when the awakening does come there is "joy unspeakable and full of glory," this is not the case of the preparatory days. Then, there is no song, but rather groans; there is no laughter, but only tears.

The first known outburst of the work of God in connection with the revival in Wales took place, strange to say, in Scranton, Pennsylvania, where a Welsh pastor with a thriving church was thrilling his audiences with his fine oratory and intellect. Suddenly this popular preacher was broken down before God to see that he was not a true prophet of the New Testament type. As a result of this true sight of himself and his seeking reality in his life, he came into a glorious experience of the fullness of the Spirit. At once his preaching took on a new note and a new power. Immediately he became burdened about his beloved Wales, and upon resigning from his church in Scranton he soon set sail for his homeland. To the consternation of the religious people in Wales who knew him before he left for America the preaching of this young minister now had a sense of urgency. No longer did he preach for effect — to stir the congregation to great heights, but he preached for results — the salvation of souls and the awakening of the Lord's people. "It was," as one has said, "indeed a strange thing to see Welsh Preaching-festivals converted into what approximated very nearly to Holiness Conventions when he was there!"

"All believed in the sincerity of the preacher; most failed to explain him; many became definitely hostile."

All this went on from 1879. The preaching of this dear brother was deeply felt among the young ministers of his own denomination. In the providence of God, early in 1903 they found themselves occupying pulpits near each other and they began to have holy fellowship with one another. This intensified their desperation to have all that God had for them and they began to be conscious of the presence of God in their midst. One of these young pastors recounts how he would be so overwhelmed after his sermon preparations on Saturday evenings that there would come upon him a mighty anointing of the Spirit which led to a period of agonizing intercession. The following day he would notice that he preached with unusual power.

Such glorious experiences beget faith and soon this little group of young ministers became definitely conscious that something glorious was going to happen in their midst.

Dr. F. B. Meyer had been greatly used to fellow-preachers in South Wales, and so they wrote to him and invited him to come and minister to them concerning the deep things of God. He replied that there would be a "Keswick Convention" at the beautiful Welsh spa of Llandridod Wells that year and invited them to attend, which they did. Here they came into an even deeper knowledge of the things of God. A mighty work was wrought in many hearts.

In August, 1904, a second convention at Llandridod Wells took place. The Spirit of God broke forth once again in glorious power during that momentous week, and none will ever forget the closing morning service when Dr. F. B. Meyer and Dr. A. T. Pierson ministered. So overcome were these dear Welsh saints with the glory of God that they sang again and again with great exuberance, "Crown Him Lord of all"!

We now turn our eyes to Cardiganshire, to a little village called New Quay, lying on the fringe of Cardigan Bay and fifteen miles from a railway station. Here the Lord had been quietly preparing instruments for the coming awakening. The Rev. Joseph Jenkins had been deeply concerned about the absence of pathos in his own voice when preaching and he desperately sought a deeper life in Christ. Dr. Andrew Murray's book *With Christ in the School of Prayer* greatly influenced his life at this time. He was greatly burdened about the indifference among all Christians around him and concerned also about the apathy of his own young people in the church. He called the young people before him and talked seriously and earnestly to them about obeying the Spirit. This was in the early part of the year 1904.

In a Sunday morning prayer meeting for young people the pastor asked for testimonies of spiritual experience. Several attempted to speak on different subjects, but the minister would not allow that. At last a young girl named Florrie Evans, who had been gloriously converted a few days before, got up, and with a tremor in her voice said, "I love Jesus Christ with all my heart."

These simple words sent a thrill throughout everyone present. The fire was ignited there, the flames of which spread soon to Blaenanerch, Newcastle-Emlyn, Capel Drindod, and Twrgwin. This was the beginning of the visible manifestations of the Spirit's breaking out in life-streams which afterwards would touch thousands of souls.

The blessing in New Quay became soon noised abroad. Doors began to open on every hand and these young people, between sixteen and eighteen years of age, led by their minister, conducted meetings throughout the south of the country. The fire was gaining strength, presently to leap forward in irresistible flames. Conventions were conducted in West Wales for holiness of heart and life in which the Spirit used mightily such men as W. S. Jones, E. Ken Evans, Jake Thickens, Seth and Frank Joshua, John Pugh, and R. B. Jones.

In August, 1904, in the city of Cardiff, the renowned evangelist R. A. Torrey held a great mission which resulted in a mighty ingathering of souls.

In November of the same year in Rhos, North Wales, the

churches invited the cultured preacher, R. B. Jones, to c
campaign there. This man had entered into the Spirit-fille(
previous year, at which time his entire ministry was chan   ...ic
now had a burning message to proclaim. A correspondent for *The
Liverpool Post* wrote concerning these meetings:

> If I had been asked a month ago whether a revival was
> probable in Wales, I should have answered no. It seemed
> to me that the higher criticism had wrecked the ordinary
> machinery of a revival and that until theology had been
> reshaped, nothing would be done to disturb the prevail-
> ing apathy.

Howbeit, in Rhos right from the very beginning, the professing
Christians were broken down before God and began to remove
the hindrances in their lives, to the full surrender to Christ and the
reception of the Spirit in His fullness. After this, the flood-gates of
heaven were opened, and the Spirit was poured out mightily. The
numbers grew until the churches were crowded out nightly. Four
weeks after our beloved brother left Rhos, a Wrexham paper said
that "the whole district is in the grip of an extraordinary spiritual
force which shows no sign of relaxing its hold."

The meetings were carried on by the people themselves, although the pastors were present. From ten o'clock in the morning
until six in the evening, the meetings went on. In the street, in the
train, in the homes, this strange power upon the town was, in hushed
and reverential tones, the theme of conversation. In the evening
after the service there were great processions marching through
the town singing hymns.

Chapter 4

THE DAWN OF A NEW DAY

As we have seen from our last chapter a new day had dawned for Wales.

God was now visiting and redeeming His people.

As many as 40,000 desperate believers, unknown to each other in the majority of cases, in various parts of the land had been waiting on the Lord and were now about to see even a greater demonstration of the mighty power of God.

Yes, it was a dark day. Everywhere the bar-rooms flourished. Football, cock-fighting, prize fighting, pigeon-flying, and betting and gambling reigned supreme especially among the working classes.

Among the chosen instruments which God in the secret place had been preparing was a young, half-educated miner who was to be the outstanding voice of his generation. It may be debated whether he was the most God-used or not, but he was by far the most known of all the preachers in this mighty awakening. Very soon the whole world would have their eyes focused on this young man.

Evan Roberts was born on June 8, 1878, in an ordinary, working-man's cottage called "Island House" in the little town of Loughor, some 210 miles from London, 50 from Cardiff, and 8 from Swansea. It is an unpretentious home, having eight very small rooms. For fifty-nine years now it has been a pilgrimage spot for the Lord's dear people from around the world, for in this house the heavens were opened to this young man.

Evan began work at a very early age in the mine. His father, Henry, broke his leg in the pit, and so his son had to help him in his job. After a few months Evan himself took up the work of a door-boy whose duty it was to look after the doors around the pit. For this he received the modest sum of seventy-five cents a week! From the coal mine he went to the trade of a blacksmith in connection with the mine.

Evan felt the burning passion to preach. His pastor and others encouraged him even though he had very little education. So, at twenty-six years of age he entered the preparatory school at Newcastle-Emlyn to prepare himself to enter the Trevecca College examination. For a long time God had been dealing with him in a most remarkable way. William Davies, a deacon at the Moriah Chapel which young Evan attended, warned him not to miss the prayer meetings in case the Holy Spirit would come and he would be missing. Thus it was that on Monday evenings he would attend the prayer meeting at Moriah, Tuesday at Pisgah, Wednesday at Moriah, and Thursday and Friday at other prayer meetings and Bible classes. He had prayed for thirteen years for a mighty visitation of the Holy Spirit.

Before going away to school, in the spring of 1904, Evan found himself, as it were, on the Mount of Transfiguration. In his own home and out on the countryside, his loving Heavenly Father revealed Himself to His child in an amazing, overwhelming manner which filled his soul with divine awe. At these special seasons every member of his body trembled until the bed was shaken. One night his brother Dan awoke and shouted, "Are you ill, Evan?" For weeks God visited his young servant in the early watches. When his family would press him to tell of these experiences he would only say it was something indescribable. When the time came near for him to enter Grammar School at Newcastle-Emlyn, he was naturally afraid to go, lest he would lose these blessed seasons with the Lord.

In the providential leadings of God, just at this time a convention was being held at Blaenanerch, some eight miles from his school. The evangelist there at the time was Rev. Seth Joshua. On Thursday morning, September 29, 1904, Evan Roberts and another nineteen young people, including his closest friend Sydney Evans, went to Blaenanerch to attend the meetings. The Lord began working in their hearts in that early morning drive as they sang "It is coming, it is coming — the power of the Holy Ghost — I receive it — I receive it — the power of the Holy Ghost."

Still singing and praising, the party of young people reached the town in time for the 7 o'clock service. Evan was deeply moved and he broke down completely when at the close of the service Mr. Joshua led in prayer. When the evangelist used the words "Bend us, oh, Lord," the soul in travail heard nothing more. "This is what *you* need," whispered the Spirit of God.

"Bend *me,* oh Lord," he cried. But even then the fire had not fallen.

"It was not Mr. Joshua who emphasized the words, 'Oh Lord, bend me', but the Spirit of God Himself," said Evan Roberts later.

At the 9 o'clock meeting the spirit of intercession was powerful. Evan was just bursting to pray. Then the Spirit of God told him to do so publicly. Let him describe this crisis experience which took place in his life at this moment, a crisis which resulted shortly in 100,000 professions of faith:

"I fell on my knees with my arms over the seat in front of me and the tears flowed freely. I cried, 'Bend me! Bend me! Bend me! Bend us.' *What 'Bent me' was God's commending His love and my not seeing anything in it to commend."*

The Holy Spirit had come and melted his whole being by the revelation to his heart of Calvary's love. Thus the theme of the entire revival became "Calvary's Love."

"But God commendeth His love toward us, in that while we were yet sinners Christ died for us" (Romans 5: 6).

He continues, "Perspiration poured down my face, and tears

streamed quickly until I thought that the blood came out. Soon, Mrs. Davies came to wipe my perspiration away. When I was in this feeling the audience sang heartily, 'I am coming now, coming, Lord, to Thee!' Now a great burden came upon me for the salvation of lost souls."

So it was, in this simple country place the longing for the fullness of the Spirit reached its maturity after fifteen years of earnest prayer. This was a never-to-be-forgotten service for Evan Roberts and for the whole of Wales; *Blaenanerch's great meeting,* he thereafter called it.

The man who was to later marry his young sister Mary, was Evan's closest companion at the school. One midnight after walking in the garden in communion with God, he came into the bedroom with a holy light on his face that astonished young Sydney. "Evan, what has happened to you?"

"Oh, Syd, I have got wonderful news for you. I had a vision of all Wales being lifted up to heaven. We are going to see the mightiest revival that Wales has ever known — and the Holy Spirit is coming just now. We must get ready. We must have a little band and go all over the country preaching."

Suddenly he stopped and with piercing eyes he looked into his friend's face. "Do you believe that God can give us 100,000 souls now?" he asked.

Sydney Evans had entered into a glorious experience with the Lord, himself, and heartily agreed with all Evan had told him. He was twenty-one years of age at this time and Evan Roberts was twenty-six.

One Sunday as he sat in the chapel at Newcastle-Emlyn, Evan could not fix his mind upon the service and ever in his mind arose in a vision the Sunday school room in his own church at Loughor. There sitting before him in the pews were his old companions and many other young people. He shook himself impatiently, trying to drive away the vision, but in vain. In his inward ear he heard a voice saying, "Go to these people."

Suddenly he said, "Lord, if it is Thy will, I will go." The whole chapel then became filled with light so dazzling that young Evan could only faintly see the minister in the pulpit. He was deeply disturbed and wanted to make sure that this vision was of the Lord, and so he consulted with his tutor who encouraged him to go.

Thus we find the young prophet, on October 31, returning to his home by train. On the train he wrote the following letter to Miss M. Cerevig Evans, a deeply spiritual young lady from Cardigan.

> Newcastle-Emlyn
> Monday morning, Oct. 31, 1904
>
> Dear Miss Evans,
> Just a line to let you know that I am on my way home for
> a week to work with our young people.
>
> The reason for this is the command of the Holy
> Spirit. He gave the command last night at the meeting.
> I could not concentrate my thoughts on the work of
> the service. I prayed and prayed so that I could follow
> the service, but of no avail. My thoughts were
> wandering, and my mind riveted on our young folk at
> Moriah. There seemed a voice, as if it said, "You must
> go, you must go!" I then told Mr. Phillips about it, and
> I asked whether it was the devil or the Spirit. He
> answered, "No, no. The devil does not give such
> thoughts. It was the voice of the Holy Spirit."
>
> Therefore, I have decided to obey, and I feel as if
> the Spirit testifies of a blessed future.
>
> And the main object of this note is to ask you and
> your friends to pray for us. I ask you in the name of
> the Saviour, to be bold at The Throne of Grace, and
> oh! endeavour to impress this indelibly on the minds
> of your friends — the importance of prayer, and
> especially on this occasion.
>
> I have written to New Quay, and have asked them to
> do the same. Oh! what a blessed band! going boldly

to The Throne of Grace!

I pray God that He will ere long pour His Spirit abundantly upon your young people.

I should like to have a word if possible from you this week. We had some awful meetings yesterday at Bethel, and a blessed meeting last night at Mr. Phillips' house.

Please excuse the lead and writing. This has been written while the train was in motion from Newcastle-Emlyn to Pencader.

Yours in the Lord,

EVAN J. ROBERTS

To my mind, this return of the young prophet to Loughor is the most thrilling of the whole story of the Welsh revival as I have heard it first-hand from the lips of his sister Mary and others of his family. His mother met him at the door and exclaimed in great surprise, "Where have you been? Why are you not at school? Are you ill!"

"No."

"Then why have you come back home?"

"Oh Mother, the Spirit has sent me back here to work among our own young people at the chapel at Moriah."

Then turning to Dan, his younger brother, he said, "You shall see that there will be a great change at Loughor in less than a fortnight. We are going to have the greatest revival that Wales has ever seen."

Evan immediately went to his pastor and asked permission to hold services for young people. On this night, after the evening adult prayer meeting, he invited the young people to stay behind as he wanted to speak to them. Alas! sixteen adults and only one little girl remained behind. This was the first "revival service," in the strict sense of the word, for Evan Roberts to conduct. Although at a loss to understand the strange ways of Evan, his mother and his two sisters, Sarah and Mary, with their brother Dan, attended. He began to explain in a very quiet voice his object in coming home. He was simply obeying the Holy Spirit, and here at Moriah he believed large numbers of young people were going to be saved. And above all, a mighty revival was coming to Wales! Thus began the most eventful meetings in Wales lasting from October 31 to November 12. Such two weeks have never been known in Wales since 1859.

Who can despise the "day of small things"? God's chosen instrument was not discouraged with the difficult beginning.

November 1.

The services were held at Pisgah, a small chapel nearby which was really a mission of Moriah. This Tuesday night the audience had greatly increased. Evan spoke on the importance of being filled with the Spirit. This meeting lasted from 7 till 10 p.m.

November 2.

Back in Moriah, Evan spoke for the first time on "The Four Great Tenets" which formed such an important part in his message at the beginning of the revival. They became known later as "The Four Points":

Did they desire an outpouring of the Spirit? Very well. Four conditions must be observed, and they were essential:

I. Is there any sin in your past that you have not confessed to God? On your knees at once. Your past must be put away and yourself cleansed.

II. Is there anything in your life that is doubtful? —anything you cannot decide whether it is good or evil. Away with it! There must not be a cloud between you and God. Have you forgiven everybody, everybody, everybody? If not, don't expect forgiveness for your own sins. You won't get it.

III. Do what the Spirit prompts you to do. Obedience — prompt, implicit, unquestioning obedience to the Spirit.

IV. A public confession of Christ as your Saviour. There is a vast difference between profession and confession.

November 3.

At this meeting he taught the children to pray, "Send the Holy Spirit to Moriah for Jesus' sake." He spoke in the evening on "Ask, and it shall be given you."

"These things must be believed," he said, "if the work is to succeed. We must believe that God is willing and able to answer our prayers. We must believe in a conquering Christ who is able to defeat all opposition."

Just as the comments on prophetic Scripture by our Saviour in His own synagogue at Nazareth astonished the hearers, so this night the church members who had known Evan all his life sat in amazement at the gracious words which proceeded out of his mouth.

November 4.

After speaking for awhile, he threw the meeting open for prayer and testimony. This went on till midnight.

November 5.

Although the meeting was announced for young people it was attended now also by the fathers and mothers, as the older people were astonished to hear of the marvelous conversions of their children. Once again Evan spoke on Ephesians 5:18. This meeting lasted from 7 p.m. till 12: 30 a.m.

The young prophet now saw the vision he had received being fulfilled before his eyes. At first the word did not seem to penetrate the hearts and consciences of the young people and the meetings were even cold. But now the whole atmosphere had changed completely.

November 6, Sunday.

To my mind this was a most remarkable day. An ordained clergyman from another town occupied the morning pulpit, as such had been arranged beforehand. Young Evan sat and listened to the message. The reader must remember that these meetings, which were to mark the mightiest manifestation of the revival, were neither advertised nor organized. The pastor was simply giving the young man Evan an opportunity to obey God in giving his witness. On this Lord's Day morning it was announced that Evan would preach in the evening.

That evening the subject of the revivalist was "The Importance of Obedience." He emphasized the following:

"I commit this meeting into the hands of the Holy Spirit. Remember, the Holy Spirit is not "something," but a Person. By giving the meeting into His hands I give it into the hands of a Person."

At the close of his message, some sixty young people responded for salvation. Then he taught the people to pray, "Send the Spirit now for Christ's sake."

This meeting lasted until well past midnight and left its mark on the whole of Loughor, for it thrilled the neighborhood with divine awe. This was the turning point of the series of meetings.

November 7.

The ordinary Monday evening prayer meeting was announced to be held at 7 o'clock as usual, and this time the old Moriah chapel was filled to the door, a thing that never occurred in the history of the prayer meeting before. At 8 o'clock the revivalist arrived. He opened the Bible and read the last chapter of the prophecy of Malachi. The people again were astonished at his holy boldness as he emphasized that this blessed Scripture was going to be fulfilled right now in Loughor in Wales!

"But unto you that fear my name, shall the sun of righteousness arise with healing in his wings, and ye shall tread down the wicked: for they shall be as ashes under the soles of your feet in the day that I shall do this, saith the Lord of hosts."

Almost all were moved to tears, and many cried in agony. It was in this meeting that the "Revival Love-song" was first sung — "Here is love, vast as the ocean."

About twelve o'clock the atmosphere became intolerable for a time and the meeting was boiling with fervor. It was 3 a.m. before any attempt at closing was possible.

November 8.

The meeting on this evening was quite cold, and the young preacher, with others, agonized fervently in prayer for God to melt the atmosphere with Calvary's love. Between 3 and 4 o'clock on Wednesday morning, some left the chapel, among whom was the preacher's mother. He followed her in order to close the door. (These weeks he could not bear the door open, as he felt the world enter at once). At the door he asked his mother, "Are you going home now, Mother?"

"Yes," she answered.

"It is better for you to come back," said he, "the Spirit comes nearer now."

"The people are sleeping," she replied, "and it will soon be time for them to go to their work."

His mother went home, undoubtedly with a heavy heart, owing to the hardness of the meeting and the strange ways of her son.

Between 6 and 7 o'clock this Wednesday morning, Dan and Evan arrived home and went to bed, but between 10 and 11 o'clock Evan was suddenly awakened by a voice. "Oh! I am dying! I am dying! I am dying!"

He swiftly got up and ran downstairs and saw his mother with clasped hands, closed eyes and great agony of soul. Having gazed upon her face, he diagnosed her case and understood her burden. Thereupon he threw his arm around her and prayed and sang with her.

"What weighed on my mind," she said later, "after leaving the chapel, was the thought of His agony in the Garden and my not staying in the chapel until the end of the service."

The whole community was now shaken. At 6 a.m. the people would be awakened by the sound of the crowds going to the early morning prayer meeting. The entire population of the town was being transformed into a praying multitude.

November 9.

Evan Roberts preached at Brynteg Congregational Chapel.

November 10.

The revival meeting was held at Brynteg again. At this meeting the audience was completely carried away by spiritual emotion. It was on this day that the first public reference to these remarkable scenes was made in a secular paper, which from this day onward for several months devoted almost the entire paper to the amazing scenes taking place in their midst. A short article appeared in *The Western Mail of Cardiff*. We know the readers will treasure it as it was the first of thousands which would come later in papers all over the world.

Great Crowds of People Drawn to Loughor
Congregations Stay Till Half-past-two
in the Morning.

A remarkable religious revival is now taking place at Loughor. For some days a young man named Evan Roberts, a native of Loughor, has been causing great surprise at Moriah Chapel. The place has been beseiged by dense crowds of people unable to obtain admission. Such excitement has prevailed that the road on which the chapel is situated has been lined with people from end to end. Roberts, who speaks in Welsh, opens his discourse by saying that he does not know what he is going to say but that when he is in communion with the Holy Spirit, the Holy Spirit will speak, and he will simply be the medium of His wisdom. The preacher soon after launches out into a fervent and, at times, impassioned oration. His statements have had most stirring effects upon his listeners. Many who have disbelieved Christianity for years are again returning to the fold of their younger days. One night, so great was the enthusiasm invoked by the young revivalist that, after his sermon which lasted two hours, the vast congregation remained praying and singing until two-thirty in the morning! Shop-keepers are closing early in order to get a place in the chapel, and tin and steel workers throng the place in their working clothes.

November 11.

Moriah is overcrowded again with some 800 people overflowing into the old chapel. Many were on their knees for a long time, owing to their distress and agony of soul. A young girl in her early teens cried out, "Oh, what will Heaven be like if it is so wonderful down here!"

November 12, Saturday.

This is an amazing day in the history of the small town of Loughor. Prayer meetings were held in the homes of the people. The longing for the salvation of their loved ones was uncontrollable. There was only one theme of conversation, and that was the glories of their wonderful Lord.

By early afternoon wagons and carts drove into town from all the surrounding countryside, and the meeting houses were overcrowded hours before the time for which the meeting had been announced. Both chapels were crowded, with Sydney Evans preaching in one and Evan Roberts in the other. In this meeting the voice of Sam Jenkins, the Welsh gospel singer, was first heard in revival. Failing to restrain his feelings, he broke out singing from the gallery, "Saved by Grace." The words of this hymn were sung by the people again and again. Also for the first time in the Welsh revival, on this night "Throw out the Lifeline" was sung.

Evan was brimming with joy as he announced, "God has brought Sydney Evans home from school to take care of the meetings here." He, himself, was leaving now for Aberdare where he had been invited to speak.

It was past 5 a.m. Sunday morning when the people dispersed, and Evan was not in bed at all, although he had to start very soon for Aberdare.

On this day all the grocery shops in town were cleared of food. The people had come from long distances, had lost all consciousness of time, and had no inclination to go home!

November 13-15, Trecynon, Aberdare.

This Sunday morning, Evan Roberts and five young ladies (Priscilla Watkins, Mary Davies, Livinia Hooker, Annie M. Rees, and Anne Davies) were driven with horse and coach by Mr. David Hughs of Loughor to meet the train at Swansea for Aberdare. These young ladies were from nearby Gorseinon and had each entered into a blessed experience of the Spirit-filled life. They were to carry the flame of the revival all over Britain during the next eighteen months.

The opening meeting on Sunday was a disappointment. The Spirit was grieved because of the criticism of the Christians against the youthful revival party. What could these young women of eighteen and twenty years of age know and tell of the deep things of the Lord?

On Monday, Ebenezer Congregational Chapel in Aberdare was crowded with one thousand people. There was no sign in this service of anything exceptional. But on Tuesday the whole neighborhood was aroused and people remained home from their work so they could attend the early morning prayer meeting, which lasted for four hours. Immense crowds gathered from all directions. In the evening service, young Evan gave out an opening hymn which was to become one of the glorious seven hymns of the revival:

> Heavenly Jesus, ride victorious,
> Gird Thy sword upon Thy thigh.

There was a spontaneous outburst of prayer and praise. The revivalist walked through the chapel clapping his hands with holy ecstasy. When the meeting was in an intense state, Roberts clearly and positively proclaimed that a mighty revival was coming to all Wales and they in Aberdare were only opening the gates for it. By the end of these meetings, the whole of Wales and Britain knew that the Holy Sprit had come to the Principality.

From Aberdare the young prophet went to Pontycymmer, a mining town in Garw one of the western valleys of Glamorganshire; then to Bridgend, Abercynon, Mountain Ash, Ynysybwl, Cilfynydd, Porth, Treorchy, Pentre, Caerphilly, Ferndale Mardy, Tylorstown, Merthyr Vale, Pontypridd, Clydach Vale, Tonypandy, Penygraig, Treherbert, Clydach, Morriston, and then on to the great industrial city of Swansea. From there he traveled on to the other surrounding parts.

It was plainly evident now to everybody that God had answered the agonizing prayers of His people and had sent a mighty spiritual upheaval. A sense of the Lord's Presence was everywhere. His Presence was felt in the homes, on the streets, in the mines, factories and schools and even in the drinking saloons. So great was His Presence felt that even the places of amusement and carousal became places of holy awe. Many were the instances of men's entering taverns, ordering drinks and then turning on their heels and leaving them untouched. Wales up to this time was in the grip of football fever when tens of thousands of working-class men thought and talked only of one thing. They also gambled on the results of the games. Now the famous football players themselves got converted and joined the open-air street meetings to testify what glorious things the Lord had done for them. Many of the teams were disbanded as the players got converted and the stadiums were empty. Beneath the ground the miners gathered for worship and Bible study before they dispersed to the various sections of the mines. Even the children in the schools came under the spell of God.

Chapter 5

THE SILENT WEEK
(February 23 to March 3, 1905)

During the space of three months before the mighty outburst of revival in Loughor, the young prophet enjoyed glorious communion with his heavenly Father. During this time he had very little sleep, for the burden of his beloved Wales prostrated him low at the Throne of Grace. Besides this, there was the overwhelming joy of the sweet seasons of fellowship in the secret place. Then during the months following the outbreak he could scarcely find time to eat or sleep, as tens of thousands crowded the villages and towns wherever it was known that he would appear. By the end of February, 1905, he must have been exhausted in mind and body.

It was at this time that the Spirit revealed to him that he must have a week of silence, no doubt for fresh instructions and anointings for further ministry. On February 22, Evan Roberts reached Godre'r-graig Neath, a little before the time when he should fulfill an engagement at Briton Ferry. It was evident that he was under a great burden. Soon he made it known that he was not going to preach — that the Spirit had ordered him to be silent. With the kind permission of his host and hostess, Mr. and Mrs. Jones, he remained confined to his bedroom without speaking to anyone, not even his loved ones. All that passed between him and the outside world during these days was done in writing. Hundreds of people, including famous preachers and newspaper men from all over the world, called to see him in the house on these days, but Mr. and Mrs. Jones refused to let anyone go to his room, in accordance with strict instructions.

Though after this time of isolation he was the same Evan Roberts, it was noted that he had an added deep stratum. This unusual incident reveals to every student of revival that a spiritual revolution is a deep and solemn affair. One's entire life and personality lies naked before a holy God for the transforming work of the Spirit.

While we will never know what really took place during this silent week, we do know from his spiritual diary that he received great onslaughts from the powers of darkness and that, like the Savior, he conquered. Some extracts from his diary during the fifth and sixth days of the "silent week" are significant:

Fifth Day—A Dedication

"I must take great care, first, to do all that God says — commands — and that only. Moses lost himself here — struck the rock. Second, to take every matter, however insignificant, to God in prayer. Joshua lost himself here; he made a covenant with the Gibeonites who pretended that they lived in a far-off country while they were living close at hand. Third, to give obedience to the Holy Spirit. Fourth, to give all the glory to Him."

Sixth Day—A Prophecy

— Lo, I am the Lord, who hath lifted thee up from the depth. I have sustained thee thus far. Lift up thine eyes and look on the fields and, behold, they are white. Shall I suffer thee to spread a table before Mine enemies? As I live, saith the Lord, the windows of heaven shall be opened, and the rain shall come down upon the parched earth. With flowers the wilderness shall yet be decked, and the meadow land shall be the habitation of kings. The ground shall sprout and blossom in its fullness and the heavens shall look down with laughter upon hidden riches on the earth, yielding glory unto God.

Open thine hand, and I will fill it with power. Open thy mouth and I will fill it with wisdom. Open thy heart, and I will fill it with love. Look toward the west, and call thousands; toward the south, and say, "Come"; toward the north, and say, "Draw nigh." Look towards the east, and say, "Let the sun arise and shed forth its warmth. Let life spring up. Let the nations which have rejected My name live." To kings turn thyself and say, "Bend"; to knights, "Submit ye." To the priests, "Deal out judgment, pity, forgiveness. Ye islands, seas, and kingdoms, give ear unto Me, I am the Almighty. Shall I lift My rod over you? Did I not swear by the prophet Isaiah: "I have sworn by myself, the word is gone out of My mouth in righteousness, and shall not return, that unto Me every knee shall bow, every tongue shall swear"? (Isaiah 45: 23)

Later, when questioned by loving friends concerning the principle object of "The Silence," he remarked, "It was not for the sake of my mind or my body to have a rest, but for a sign. When I asked the Lord what was the object of the seven days of silence He distinctly said,

'As thy tongue was tied for seven days, so shall Satan be bound seven times.'"

Chapter 6

THE REVIVAL EVERYWHERE

Before we introduce you to a typical revival meeting, it is necessary for all who pray for revival to know the principles that govern the Spirit's working and how He will work when He is allowed to in your own local church, town and country.

The awakening in Wales teaches us many outstanding lessons, one of which is that while God uses human instruments such as Evan Roberts, He is in no way limited to the personality of one man. When Christians and the unsaved alike follow a popular preacher instead of the Lord Jesus Christ Himself, then we know that it is not a true revival.

Again, when a spiritual harvest depends almost entirely upon one personality we know that there is no true revival. *The glorious fact and outstanding feature of the mighty awakening in Wales was that the sense of the Lord's Presence was everywhere throughout the entire nation, altogether apart from the young revivalist. Glory to God! it was not the presence of Evan Roberts that was felt but the mighty presence of God. Evan Roberts was only one of the broken instruments which the Spirit of God was using.* As we have already mentioned, there were crowds of pastors and evangelists reaping mighty harvests simultaneous with the ministry of Evan and Dan Roberts, Sydney Evans, Sam Jenkins and "The Singing Sisters." For example, R. B. Jones was conducting meetings in Amlych in the Isle of Anglesey in the north of Wales in January, 1905, and found that revival had even then reached that northernmost point in Wales although young Roberts had never been there.

In Amlych, the capel mawr (big chapel) was crowded. The

theme of the preacher's message was from Isaiah, chapter 6. A tremendous sense of conviction of sin settled upon all present. The hearers were crushed beyond despair. The uppermost cry was "Could God forgive? Could God cleanse?" When the messenger came to the words telling of the "live coal from off the altar" — the cleansing fire from the place where the blood was shed, Calvary — and the live coal touching the confessedly vile lips, the effect was electrifying. One who was present at that meeting says that it was absolutely beyond any metaphor to describe. As one man stood, first with a sigh of relief and then with a delirious shout of joy, the whole audience of 1200 people simultaneously sprang to their feet shouting "Diolch Iddo!" (Thanks be to Him.) The glory of God so shone upon the pulpit that the evangelist fled to the vestry completely overcome. He could not stand the brightness of the glory of the presence of God.

In the Awakening in Wales, it was the presence of thousands of young converts exulting in the thrill of their new-found Redeemer that carried all before it. These were drunk with the new wine of the Spirit and were oblivious to everything else than their blessed Lord Jesus. Like the young converts in The Book of Acts, they went everywhere preaching the Word without the authority of man, having the ordination of the Spirit. Even little children won many souls for Christ.

Some readers may criticize such enthusiasm and call it only religious emotionalism, and yet these same critics believe in full expression of the emotions in the football stadium. I, myself, know the frenzy of the tens of thousands who pack the stadiums in Britain, as I played before them when I was beginning a professional football career. They were hypnotized and drunk with the sport. They packed the stadiums in all kinds of weather, oblivious to all the elements. Yet I found many of these same people criticizing me for being "emotionally upset" when, with burning words, I pleaded with them to accept Christ as their Savior. The world believes in emotion in the world but not in the church.

I have before me some treasured copies of *The Evening Express*, and *The Evening Mail* of Cardiff, published during these blessed days. *The Evening Express,* along with other Welsh newspapers, published a weekly paper exclusively devoted to the progress of the revival, because the revival was the biggest thing in the mind of all Wales. One page of this *Weekly* is devoted to "The Doings of the Churches" and is divided into several sections, such as Anglican, Primitive Methodists, Baptists, Y.M.C.A., Christian Endeavor, etc. The paper also carries two or three hymns with words and music. The large advertisements are devoted to the sale of Bibles and hymn books, which could be purchased from different Christian publishers in Britain. There is also a column called "Revival Harvest." These reports are compiled by different correspondents throughout Wales who seek to bring before the readers each week the movements of the Spirit. The towns appear in alphabetical order from Aberaman to Ynystawe.

From time to time there is what they call "A Revival Map of Great Britain", showing how the revival is spreading. For example, in the edition of January 18, 1905, are the following words beneath the revival map:

"The above map shows the districts affected mainly by the revival. The shading shows the degree of the intensity of the Awakening. Wales stands first, then Cornwall, then afterwards the portions lightly shaded." Many of these issues also carry revival cartoons.

Here are some of the reports from the different villages and towns throughout the nation, gleaned from several of these papers. They eloquently reveal that it was not Evan Roberts but the Lord Jesus who was the center of the attraction. The believers in Wales are intensely proud of their young prophet and woe betide anyone who seeks to criticize him, but they do not idolize him. They know that he was not the secret and cause of the success of the awakening, but only one of the chosen instruments.

DOINGS OF THE CHURCHES

Blaenavon. On Saturday evening a band of young lads between the age of 14 and 16 held prayer meetings in the different places in the principle streets.

Dowlais. At a recent prayer meeting, attended by no fewer than 214 persons, the proceedings resolved themselves into a huge Bible class. This great interest in the Holy Scriptures is the result of the present revival.

Bryncethin. The services have now been held here nightly for fifteen weeks, and a large number of converts have been added to the Free Churches. For the sake of educating the young converts it has been decided to have a Bible class for two nights in every week and these classes are very largely attended.

Rhos. Visitors to the revival meeting continue to pour in from the Lake District; Birkenhead, Liverpool, and the adjoining districts.

Tremadoc. The revival has had and continues to have a marked effect here. *The chapels have been overflowing up to two and three o'clock in the morning.*

Newbridge. An official of the Colynen colliery, when asked how the religious fervor had expressed itself underground, said: "This is a blessed time. When I go around on my inspection now I rarely ever hear a blasphemous word of oath. There is a glorious change for the better."

Cardigan. A meeting in the Tabernacle Calvinist Methodist Church where the Rev. Seth Joshua was conducting a mission was prolonged till after midnight. It was a wonderful gathering and will long be remembered for the outpouring of the Holy Spirit. Most of the 1,203 people present were on their knees praying simultaneously and they remained in this attitude for about 2 hours and many persons are known to have accepted Christ.

Holyhead. In this important town a drunken man is a thing of the past and the police are having an easy time of it. *Five hundred converts have been reported.*

Pontypool. The missionary enthusiasm is running high amongst the 200 converts at the Tabernacle and at a recent meeting it was decided to divide them into groups and to hold services at different cottages.

Street disturbances have become conspicuous by their absence and the fact that there has not been a single fight at the bottom of High Street, which is always regarded as the "prize ring of Pontypool," is put down to the good influences of the Revival.

Coedboeth. *This quiet neighborhood has felt a strong spiritual visitation for the past three months.* The total number of converts is now 210 and many more are expected. There have been united prayer meetings three nights a week and on the rest of the evenings each church holds meetings at its own place of worship. Remarkable scenes have been witnessed. The women have daily prayer meetings, morning and afternoon. Young men and young women are testifying in the open air with great success, and many drunkards have been converted. The life of the whole churches have been reformed.

Blaenavon. All the churches in the town recently had a combined procession through the streets and now a second parade has been arranged.

Bertillery. *As the result of the special week of meetings there have been about 1,500 converts.*

Brithoir. A meeting near the railway station — the continuation of a previous prayer meeting — was attended by many persons from clubs and public houses and continued till near midnight. Then they went to the nearby Chapel and the gathering broke up at 2 a.m.

Ammanford. Half a dozen young people cannot meet accidentally in the street without joining in praise. Recently a group of children met on The Cross and began to sing and pray. Ultimately they were joined by men and women and the result was a grand open-air prayer meeting. Ammanford is a new town. Young people, full of enthusiasm, frequently walk three or four miles over the mountains to villages, farms and hamlets to hold meetings.

Treharris. At Brynhyfryd Welsh Baptist, forty candidates were recently baptized making a total of 138 baptisms. 220 have recently been saved in this church.

Rhondda Valley. *A scene which may be witnessed any morning in dozens of pits in South Wales is carried out every morning here at 5 am.* Scores of miners hold a service before going home from the midnight shift. The Superintendent starts a hymn, "In the deep and mighty ocean", and then the pit re-echoes the song. An old man whose grey head is tinged with coal-dust falls on his knees to pray. Others do the same. The service attracts men from different workings and flickering lights are seen approaching the improvised temple. "Now, boys, those of you who love Christ, up with your lamp!" cries a young miner. In a second, scores of lights flicker in the air and another song of thanks sets the mine ringing.

Abertillery (again). The work goes on. Great things have taken place in the Salvation Army Hall but services are held nightly in practically every chapel in the neighborhood. There are now 2,500 converts.

Anglesey. The Isle of Anglesey has been stirred from end to end by the revival. At the 55 Methodist chapels there have been 1,116 converts, 276 at 15 Independent chapels, 366 at the 24 Baptist places of worship and 116 at the 8 Wesleyan Churches, *making a total of 1,673 converts for the 102 chapels.*

Carnarvon. A score of volunteer missioners numbering 150 from the local churches of the town have undertaken house to house visitation to invite the people to come to the churches.

Revival fervor in Durham (England). Revival fervor still spreads in North West Durham in the North of England. Those connected with the cause for a long period remember *no such general awakening during the last 20 years.* There has been an upheaval which has been the general topic of conversation throughout the whole district. All over Durham marvelous scenes are taking place and the chapels are packed every night with souls being saved.

Garw Valley. *Underground meetings are being held in nearly all the colleries.* The early converts are among the most ardent workers and their efforts are proving very successful. At one of these underground meetings, no fewer than 36 men surrendered themselves to Christ.

Garndiffaith. At Pisgah 40 conversions are recorded. A man 70 years of age stood up and confessed Christ as his Saviour. Although late, he felt that he was glad that he had at last found peace and joy. A young man had been praying for his father, and he asked that his petition might be answered that night. Just then his father came to the meeting and made a full surrender. A man who had been a great drunkard and blasphemer and who had starved his wife and children by missing his work for weeks at a time, found his way into one of the meetings and, with tears streaming from his eyes, he cried aloud for forgiveness. He prayed that God might find a way to his wife's heart and she, too, soon cried for pardon. Shouts of praise and joy were raised.

Glynneath. *The two independent churches Addoldy and Capel-Y-Glyn which had been on unbrotherly terms for a period of nearly twelve years have been reconciled and united meetings have been held.* The two ministers shook hands before a united church of nearly 400 members.

Hafod. Underground prayer meetings at the Trevor pit have been conducted by Mr. W. Rogers who is known as the converted footballer.

Pentre. The ministers of all the chapels recently exchanged pulpits for a day with the idea of breaking down denominationalism.

Maesteg. An insurance agent told a reporter that at practically every house he called at after Christmas he was met by the wife with a happy smile and these words, "This is the happiest Christmas we have ever had." Their husbands had been converted and stopped their wastage of money in gambling and drunkenness.

Carnarvon. Details have just reached us of wonderful meetings. The influence of the Holy Spirit is felt most powerfully by men and women alike. *Strong men pale and tremble.* Young men and women storm the gates of heaven with overwhelming importunity and overpowering effect. The whole congregation is completely melted into pronounced weeping and sobbing. Large numbers are finding the Lord. Two well-known reprobates came forward and sank on their knees and began to beat their breasts.

The Bible Society's records show that over three times the number of Bibles are now being sold since the revival broke out. The book-sellers say it is no trouble now to sell Bibles; the trouble is to *get* them.

A lovely story is told of a child of four in an infant class who held up his hand to call the teacher's attention.

'Well?" inquired the teacher, "What is it?"

Swift and telling came the words, "Please, teacher, do you love Jesus?"

The arrow reached its mark. There and then the teacher came to the Lord, and she later went out to India as a missionary.

Someone overheard one child ask another, "Do you know what has happened at Rhos?"

"No, I don't, except that Sunday comes every day now!"

"Don't you know?"

"No, I don't."

"Why, Jesus Christ has come to live in Rhos, now."

Longstanding debts were paid, stolen goods returned,

drinking taverns forsaken, oaths ceased to be heard so that it was said in the mines the horses could not understand the language of their drivers. Political meetings had to be postponed as members of the Houses of Parliament were found taking part in the revival meetings. Theatrical companies made sure that they did not come to Wales as they knew that there they would go bankrupt. Magistrates were presented with white gloves in many places to signify that there were no arrests. The prisons were empty. Even in the universities, revival scenes were commonplace day after day for months.

The mighty tidal wave swept through the land. The Spirit of God found His own channels, and districts which were never reached by Evan, Dan, or Sydney, had extraordinary manifestations of the power of God. I have before me, as I write, my cherished copies of some newspapers of that day in which were posted each week a tabulated form of the lists of converts in each town for that week. Over 70,000 names of converts are reported just two months after the lifestreams broke out!

Words on Memorial Stone
"The Lord has visited and redeemed His People"!

Moriah where mighty scenes took place.

Dan Roberts

Sydney Evans

Evan Roberts

The House where the Revivalist was born and where he had extra ordinary communion with God.

Chapter 7

A REVIVAL MEETING

It is difficult for us almost sixty years later to trace the ministry of all the dear servants of God who were so mightily used at this time. As suggested before, so great was the glory of God manifested to them that they felt totally insignificant and unworthy. What a pity it is that men like Seth Joshua, R. B. Jones, and others did not publish a modest report of all that God had wrought in their meetings. *Because of this silence, there are at least one hundred books unwritten on the Welsh Revival.* Only the "Bema" of Christ will reveal the great exploits of ordinary men and women of God in that day.

Evan Roberts was by far the most publicized preacher of the day. This was not of his own seeking. He was deeply distressed at all the publicity he was receiving and he soon decided that his movements must not be announced beforehand. On many occasions when it was known where he would preach, he would simply say to the ministers who invited him, "Yes, I believe the Lord would have me accept your invitation and come for three days, but please do not announce in what building I will preach, the people must come for the Lord and Him alone; otherwise the Holy Spirit will withdraw Himself from our midst."

The revivalist also was extraordinarily careful that it should not be thought that the work depended on him.

"I am only one of the instruments God is using. There are many others," he would say. "It is true that God gave me a vision and God gave me a call to this revival, but it was a joy for me to discover later that the same experience was duplicated in the lives of so many dear saints of God. Unknown to each other the same

Spirit of God had burdened us all for this awakening."

"People must not rely on me," was his constant cry. "I have nothing for them. They must rely on Him Who alone can minister to their needs. When you go to the window, you do not go to look at the glass, but *through* it at the scenery beyond. Then look through me and see the Lord."

It is easier for us to trace the supernatural work of the Spirit in the meetings of young Roberts, however, owing to the heavy publicity that his meetings received.

Time limits in the meetings were forgotten. Announced to begin a certain hour, people gathered an hour or two before. Meetings closed when they were ended. Clocks were completely ignored. Meetings began as soon as part of the congregation had assembled. There was no waiting for any human leader. Never was there a religious movement so little indebted to the guiding brains of its leaders. When the evening meeting which began at 7 o'clock poured out at 3 o'clock next morning other crowds were preparing to get into the chapel for the early morning prayer meeting! In many places all work ceased during the time of the visit of Evan Roberts. The factories and shops sometimes closed for one to three days so the people could attend the meetings.

A famous reporter of the great *London Daily* visited the meetings of the young prophet of Loughor in order to describe to the people in London the amazing scenes about which they had heard. He wrote:

> I found the flame of Welsh religious enthusiasm as smokeless as its coal. There are no advertisements, no brass bands, no posters. All the paraphernalia of the got-up job are conspicuous by their absence. There is no instrumental music. The pipe organs lie unused. There is no need of instruments for in and around and beneath surge the all-prevailing thrill and throb of a multitude praying, and singing as they pray.
>
> The vast congregations are soberly sane, as orderly

and at least as reverent as any congregation I ever saw beneath the dome of St. Paul's cathedral. Tier above tier in the crowded aisle to the loftiest gallery sit or stand as necessity dictates, eager hundreds of serious men and thoughtful women, their eyes riveted upon the platform or upon whatever part of the building is the storm center of the meeting. The vast majority of the congregation are stalwart young miners.

"We must obey the Spirit" is the watchword of Evan Roberts, and he is as obedient as the humblest of his audience. No one uses a hymn book; no one gives out a hymn. The last person to control the meeting in any way is Evan Roberts. You feel that the thousand or fifteen hundred persons before you have become merged into one myriad-headed but single-souled personality. You can watch what they call "the influence of the power of the Spirit playing over the congregation as an ebbying wind plays over the surface of the pond.

A very remarkable instance of this abandonment of the meeting to the spontaneous impulse, not merely of those within the walls but of those crowded outside, who were unable to get in, occurred on Sunday night. Twice the order of proceeding, if order it can be called, was altered, by the crowd outside who, by some mysterious impulse started a hymn on their own account which was at once taken up by the congregation within. On one of these occasions Evan Roberts was addressing the meeting. He at once gave way and the singing became general.

The meeting always breaks out into a compassionate and consoling song, until the soloist, having recovered his breath, rises from his knees and sings a song.

The praying and singing are both wonderful. But more impressive than either are the breaks which occur when utterance can no more, and then the sobbing in the silence momentarily heard is drowned in tempest of melody. No need for an organ. The assembly is its own organ as a thousand or fifteen hundred sorrowing or rejoicing hearts find expression in the sacred Psalmody of their native hills.

Repentance, open confession, intercessory prayer, and above all else this marvelous musical liturgy — a liturgy unwritten, but heart-felt — a mighty chorus rising like the thunder of the surge of the rock-bound shore, ever and anon broken by the flute-like note of the singing sisters whose melody is as sweet and as spontaneous as the music of the throstle in the grove or the martin in the skies. And all this vast quivering, throbbing, singing, praying, exultant multitude intensely conscious of the all-pervading influence of some invisible reality — now for the first time moving palpable though not tangible in their midst.

They call it the Spirit of God.

Naturally, when the young revivalist went to new places where the people had never seen nor heard him before and many had even come from distant lands, it was only to be expected that they would pack out the meetings in expectation that he would be there. Such was the case in Liverpool, for instance. Said Sir Edward Russell, the distinguished journalist and editor of the *Liverpool Post*:

If anyone had gone into the great Calvinist church in the Princess Row on the Saturday evening without any previous intimations, he might well have failed to discover — at all events till after four hours — and then he might have been forgiven for missing it — that the 2500 densely-packed, visibly excited people assembled had come to hear and were longing to hear, a young man who in the main sat saying nothing, doing nothing, with his head on his hands.

Let us visit together a typical revival service.

A spiritual cyclone has already swept the town even before the revivalist's visit. Thirteen hundred newborn souls are rejoicing in their great Redeemer. The service has been going on for three hours without any human leader. Nobody can say who started the service and nobody can say even at this moment how the service is going to continue. They are singing with great intensity:

> See! the Righteous Sun is risen
>   O'er our land in splendour bright:
> Every desert part now liveth —
>   Verdue green gives forth delight.
> Jesu's Spirit is still rushing
>   As the wind, with strength and flame;
> Sinners seek, in deep repentance,
>   Free salvation in His Name.
>
> Hush! I hear the winds re-echoing
>   Jesu's words on Calvary:
> "It is finished"; for the sinner
>   Life, salvation, liberty:
> Jesus Christ, the great Redeemer,
>   At the Throne now pleads for thee;
> O, ye sinners, do receive Him,
>   He will save and set you free.

Now an earnest lad of sixteen years comes straight up to the front of the audience with a Bible in his hand waiting for a break in the meeting. He stands silent with rapt expression and then when he reads the portion in Welsh he slips away. He has obeyed the Spirit.

A young miner just converted two weeks before cannot keep still. He just has to break forth in song. Thus he begins to sing:

> Hast thou ever heard of the Savior of men,
>   That willingly died on the tree?
> He gave Himself as an offering for sin,
>   He suffered and suffered for thee;
> He died on the cross, but He rose from the grave,
> A Savior that's able and willing to save.
>
> Hast thou ever heard of the sinless and true,
>   Who pities a sinner like thee?

51

Did father or mother to child ever tell
  Of any so gracious as He?
He healeth the sick and restoreth the blind,
To all that accept Him the Savior is kind.

O sinner, come to Him, He calleth for thee,
  A prodigal life lead no more;
He seeketh to save thee from sin and from death,
  He's knocking even now at thy door:
Accept Him this moment, it is not too late,
Thy sin He will pardon, although it is great.

In prayer continue, He will hear thy voice,
  For thee in thy weakness He pleads;
In glory, He has not forgotten thee, friend,
  But for thee in love intercedes.
Forgiveness, forgiveness, He'll freely bestow,
And make thee, poor sinner, even whiter than snow

      O, for thee He is waiting,
      O, for thee He is waiting,
      O, for thee He is waiting just now.

The young man can only get through the first verse before he
breaks into sobbing. Spontaneously the people all over the building take up and continue the invitation hymn. The chorus is sung
some thirty or forty times by all the people. The building is filled
with the glory of the Lord. Every eye beams an unusual radiance.
Each bosom swells with the surge of feeling.

A young lady now stands. She is Annie Davies with the night-
ingale voice. She is only eighteen years of age. Previously she had
come with her sister to a revival service in a critical and cold attitude for she was out of touch with the Lord. Not so tonight; she is
completely broken down. Her soul is moved to its deepest depths.
She cannot refrain from weeping. With an irresistible force her
voice begins to flood the whole building with what later would be
known as "The Love Song" of the revival:

Wondrous Love, unbounded Mercy!
  Vast as oceans in their flood:
Jesus, Prince of Life, is dying
  Life for us is in His blood!
Oh! What heart can e'er forget Him?
  Who can cease His praise to sing?
Wondrous Love! forever cherished
  While the Heavens with music ring.

Now comes Evan Roberts, quietly elbowing his way through the dense crowd which throngs the aisle and the chapel, and leans over the big Bible on the pulpit desk. He waits silently for some time and then begins to pray:

Lord Jesus, help us now through the Holy Spirit to come face to face with the cross. Whatever the hindrances may be, we commit the service to Thee. Put us all under the Blood. Oh, Lord, place the Blood on all our past up to this moment. We thank Thee for the Blood. In the Name of Jesus Christ bind the devil this moment. We point to the Cross of Christ. It is our Cross and we take its conquest. Reveal the Cross through the Name of Jesus. Oh, open the Heavens. Descend upon us now. Tear open our hearts — tear — give us such a sight of Calvary that our hearts may be broken. Oh Lord, descend now…now…open our hearts to receive the heart that bled for us. If we are to be fools — make us fools for Thee. Take us, spirit, soul, and body. We are Thine. Thou hast purchased us. Reveal the Cross for the sake of Jesus —the Cross that is to conquer the world. Place us under the Blood. Forbid that we should think of what men may say of us. Oh speak — speak — speak, Lord Jesus. Thy Words are "wine indeed." Oh, reveal the Cross, beloved Jesus — the Cross in its glory. Reign in every heart for the sake of Jesus. Lord, do Thou help us to see the dying Saviour. Enable us to see Him conquering the hosts of darkness. Claim victory for Thy Son, now Lord. He is worthy to have the victory.

Thou art the all-powerful God. Oh, claim victory. We shall give all the glory to Thy Name. No one else has a right to the glory but Thee. — Take it, Lord. Glorify Thy Son in this meeting. Oh, Holy Spirit — do thou work through us and in us now. Speak Thy Word in power for Thy Name's sake. Amen — and Amen!

All around, the huge audience of men and women begin to pray and heaven is opened as different people stand up in different parts of the building, down below and in the gallery, crying out, "Lord, save me!" "Oh God, I come to Thee now!' This is followed by shouts of glory echoing through the building and then, as if an invisible conductor had come to the pulpit with his baton, the crowd now sings exultingly with glorious triumph:

> Ride in triumph, blessed Jesus,
>   Gird Thou on Thine armour bright,
> Neither earth can stand before Thee,
>   Nor proud hell with all its might;
> At Thy name, so great and glorious,
>   All Thy foes depart in fear;
> Terror holds the wide creation
>   When Thou, Christ of God, art near.

The revivalist has been waiting for the Spirit's time for him to give the message. He begins now his message. It is on the "Sufferings of Christ." He is not long speaking when he himself is broken down. He tries *again* to picture the depths of the suffering Savior.

He is not allowed to continue as a young girl thrills the assembly when she cries out, "Oh, dear Jesus, sweating for me!" The people are quite overcome and are bathed in tears. There is a subdued holy quietness now over the atmosphere while hundreds, unsaved and saved alike, whisper in holy wonder, "Oh, blessed Lord Jesus, Who died for me."

Now, one by one, people stand up and testify of being saved there and then.

Someone suddenly commences a hymn. The scene is suddenly changed. The whole crowd is on its feet now, swayed by intense spiritual enthusiasm, and pouring out its feelings in various ways — a word of praise, a hymn of spiritual worship, a Bible message from an unknown person.

Visitors who have come from all parts of the world to see this amazing sight and who have never been in a revival meeting before cry out, "Hush!" They have come to hear Evan Roberts. But what is the good of saying "Hush"? It would have been as well to say "hush" to the ocean's swelling tide. The deepest emotions of the people have been liberated, and they rush forth like a mighty flood.

A beautiful voice begins now to sing. It comes from the gallery. It is Sam Jenkins, the singing evangelist. "Tell Mother I'll be there…" rings out in song:

> Tell Mother I'll be there
> In answer to her prayer:
> This message, blessed Savior, to her bear.
> Tell Mother I'll be there,
> Heav'n's joys with her to share…
> Yes, tell my darling mother I'll be there.

Once again the revivalist tries to speak, but a thin piping voice in the gallery begins to unburden its soul.

"Shh! Shh," cries the congregation, listening for the voice of the evangelist.

In a moment, with a wave of the hand, he stops the rebuking voices and waits till that small, quivering treble ceases. We are reminded of One of whom the prophet foretold, "The smoking flax will He not quench."

The spirit of intercession is once again poured out. *Almost a hundred persons are on their feet engaged in prayer at one time and yet everything seems to be in perfect harmony.* All are gloriously conscious of the wonderful presence of Jehovah in their midst. Evan Roberts is now radiantly happy. The handsome face, the arresting eye, the gentle voice infused with an emotional tremor, all bespeak the love of the Spirit.

Thus the meeting goes on until 3 o'clock next morning.

Chapter 8

THE EFFECTS OF THE REVIVAL

The effects of the revival in Wales were astonishing. For example, the correspondent for *The Liverpool Daily Post* reported in December, 1904, that there had been no arrests for drunkenness in Rhos since the revival had started. The earnings of the workmen, instead of being squandered in drink and vice, were now bringing great joy to their families. Outstanding debts were being paid by thousands of young converts. Restitution was the order of the day.

The gambling and alcohol businesses lost their trade and the theatres closed down from lack of patronage. Football during this time was forgotten by both players and fans, though nothing was mentioned from the pulpits about the evils of football. In this country which had a general reputation of being "football mad," the train for taking the crowds to the international trial match was found to be almost empty! The people had a new life and new interests.

The famous singing festivals of Welsh culture which were always so popular in the land somehow in these wonderful days sickened and died. The trained professional vocalists of Wales became singing "Sankeys" and "Alexanders" who came forth now with such hymns as "Throw Out the Lifeline" while the glory of God filled their souls. Even the few concerts which remained usually closed with both singers and audience singing together the songs which had become popular during the revival, such as "Tell Mother I'll be There," "Ride in Triumph, Blessed Jesus," "Who is a Pardoning God Like Thee," etc.

Political meetings were cancelled or abandoned. They seemed

completely out of the question since nobody was interested. The political leaders, even from the parliament in London, abandoned themselves to the revival meetings.

One of the most significant results was that the old church prejudices were broken down. The man-made denominational barriers completely collapsed as believers and pastors of all denominations worshipped their majestic Lord together. The quarrels of local Christians were healed. One of the outstanding features of the revival was the confession of sin, not among the unsaved alone, but among the saved. All were broken down and melted before the cross of Christ.

The revival and the effects which followed in its wake could not be kept local. Revival is like a prairie fire which carries all before it. It breaks out here and there in the most unexpected places to the amazement of everyone. It is not surprising then that the mighty fire which engulfed the nation of Wales soon spread to different parts of the earth. Visiting preachers and ordinary believers who had come to see the sights of "the burning bush" returned home to start *fires* in their own church, mission field, and city. God's people all over the world began to shout for joy.

As was to be expected, the first to feel the fire of revival were the Welsh-speaking colonies in America and elsewhere. In far-off India the fire swept through the Welsh mission fields. All of Britain as well as the Continent began to be invaded for Christ by scores of evangelists, pastors, Bible teachers, and even laymen who had either been converted or had "caught the fire" in Wales during the revival. I myself have labored with some of these blessed men of God and know that even to this day the work still stands. One preacher, for example, whose life was revolutionized took the revival fire to a Scandinavian country where today there is at least one hundred churches flourishing as a direct outcome of his ministry. Rev. and Mrs. Rees Howells are examples of evangelists who took the fire of God to the mission field. They saw God work in an amazing way in South Africa, and returned later to found the Bible College of South Wales in Swansea from which missionaries would go to the ends of the earth.

A young Latvian student from Spurgeon's College in London broke away from his classes on hearing of the fire of God in Wales and made a bee-line to Swansea. There he caught the flame. The Spirit of God came upon him mightily so that when he returned to his beloved Russia he carried the flame of revival to that land. As I labored with this man for many years I was conscious of the lasting effect of the Welsh revival upon his ministry. Not only did he lead tens of thousands to Christ, but he was instrumental in building some two hundred churches in Eastern Europe.

The year 1905 will never be forgotten in the history of the English Keswick Convention. It came to be known as *"The Welsh Week"* as many young pastors came from Wales to tell what God had done in their churches. In one meeting of three hours there was not a break in spontaneous praise, confession, and worship. Friday night was an outstanding occasion when E. W. Moore was giving a message from I Corinthians 3:11-15 on "The Ordeal of Fire," dwelling on the necessity of building upon the right foundation with purified materials and the possibility of the Christian himself being saved while his works are burnt up by the fire of God.

Dr. R. B. Jones writes of this message:

> *I felt God's refining fire go through me, revealing the wood, hay, and stubble of work and motive. When I arose to speak, so humbling and overwhelming was this conviction that when called upon to lead in prayer and address the meeting, it was quite involuntary that I should first of all make my confession. I did so and asked others who, like me, had felt conscious of God's direct dealing, to stand with me before God as those who, then and there, besought Him to refine us now that worthless material might not accumulate against the coming "Day of fire."*

The invitation was so responded to that the whole tent full of people rose as one man! Not one word of the proposed address carefully prepared for this closing meeting was ever delivered. It had been my intention to speak on "Praying in the Holy Spirit."

As Prebendary Webb-Pebloe well said, "God had no need for the sermon as He proposed giving an illustration of the theme instead!"

I stood there on my feet for about 2 ½ hours witnessing the Holy Spirit's working. God moved in wholly unexpected ways and no one could think of interfering. It is quite obvious that He had set aside chairman and speaker and was both presiding and speaking Himself. A strange hush of God was on the meeting. The service closed with a great burst of adoration to our wonderful God as we sang, "All hail the power of Jesu's Name and crown Him Lord of all!"

Chapter 9

WHY THE FIRE FELL

If it be asked why the fire of God fell on Wales, the answer is simple. Fire falls where it is likely to catch and spread. As one has said, "Wales provided the necessary tinder." Here were thousands of believers unknown to each other, in small towns and villages and great cities, crying to God day after day for the fire of God to fall. This was not merely a "little talk with Jesus" but daily agonizing intercession. They had also placed the wood upon the altar and had fully surrendered to the claims of their Redeemer. They had a holy jealousy for the name of their God and wept sorely because of the fact that Satan was being glorified all around them. They constantly reminded God of what He had done in the past — in 1859. "Oh Lord, Thou art the same," they cried, "and Thou canst do it again —even in this industrious, luxurious age."

It is good also to remember that the theme of the young prophet of Loughor, "bend the church and save the world," is the secret of every true awakening. Christians must humble themselves and get right with God so that the Spirit can break through in converting power upon the unsaved. There must be no hypocrisy; the Christian must bend to all the will of God for His life in perfect obedience before the Spirit of God is released.

The Holy Spirit was recognized and honored as a divine Person. They obeyed Him immediately without any reservation. Thus they received holy anointings and they swept on as a conquering army.

Oh God, send the fire once again!

Chapter 10

A MESSAGE OF EVAN ROBERTS'

"Now the Lord had said unto Abraham, Get thee out of thy country, and from thy kindred, and from thy father's house, unto a land that I will show thee; and I will make of thee a great nation, and I will bless thee, and make thy name great; and thou shalt be a blessing" — Gen. 12: 1, 2.

We all ought to obey God as Abraham obeyed Him. What was Abraham? What was his knowledge of God? What amount of revelation had he received from God as compared with us? He was an idolater, and God called him to leave his country, his nation, his father's home. What shall follow this? "I will make thee a great nation." "I will magnify thy name" — he shall be a magnet, a man full of God, who shall draw everybody unto him. And Christ said, "I, if I be lifted up, shall draw all men unto Me." All must be filled with the Spirit of God if they are to draw men to them. It may be unconsciously, but the Spirit-filled man draws them. If a man is a friend of God, everything in him draws — silence draws, everything he does draws. He cannot but draw. The magnet cannot help it; and only the magnet draws. We must be in readiness to give obedience to God. If Abraham obeyed without much knowledge of God, should not we obey, to whom so much has been revealed?

We should give obedience instantly. God calls every one of us, but people are so stupid. But thank God! there are many now through all the world who obey, not only the voice, but the authority behind it, and thereby see more clearly. God not only calls, but He gives the blessings. He does not call without giving a promise. "I will make thee a great nation." "And they shall be a great nation." It is wonderful. Abraham has the blessing. He brings blessing upon men. "Those that bless thee shall be blessed." The nation goes into captivity. Is it then at an end with them? No! Heaven makes no mistake. The promise will be kept.

Where is the enemy? He thinks he is getting a big victory, but God puts his hand lightly upon the enemy. If anyone shall put his hand upon the child of God to oppose him, God will put His hand upon him. If you put your hand upon a child of God, God's hand will press you down. The oppressor's hand is upon you. Why is that so? How much has it cost God to make us His children? It cost Him putting His hand upon His own Son. Woe to him who touches the children of God! It is touching the apple of His eye.

OBEDIENCE TO THE CALL

Everyone must obey, and go where God directs him. That is the great lesson we have to learn. If God calls, we must obey. Do not ask, "What will become of me?" It does not matter what. God is a God of light. He has plenty of light to shed upon your path. "I am the light of the world." "I am weak," says a man. It does not matter. God is strong. He is a God of all power, and if God is for us, who can be against us? The path will be made light for us, so that we shall not lose our way. Nobody ever lost his way who followed Him. You must keep near to your Leader. If anyone loses his way, it is either by going too far behind or going before God. If he says, "Come after Me," we are to follow. "But the enemies are powerful." It does not matter. If ten thousand are against you, do not be afraid — God is with you. If you are filled with God, you are not afraid of anybody except God.

God has been calling for years. We have been saying, "No." If we are children of God, let us obey. What should you think of a father who had a son and asked him to do something, and he said "No!" all day; what should you think of that son? He is not worthy to be called a son because of his disobedience. But that is old history, and it is true today.

We pray "Send us power down!" There is no need. The Holy Spirit is with us. I realize that He is here. We need not pray that He should come. If you read the second chapter of Acts, you will find that He has been sent. We have an account that He came. Have you an account that He went back? Our prayer should be "Open our hearts to receive Him!" He presses hard on the door of your heart, but He cannot get in. It is open to everybody else, but not to Christ. Must He call again and again and find us disobedient? The Spirit is calling continually, but I thank God that He is here today. I am glad to find you in the Spirit today. Obey Him! Rest upon God. That will be the place for you. What joy to be in heaven resting upon Him forever! Just roll your burden upon Him. The Spirit calls continually, calls everybody. That is the danger — not heeding the voice.

NOT "SOMETHING", BUT "HIM"

Do you know what people called the Holy Spirit in the past? They called Him "something" — they knew not what. Now we call Him the Holy Ghost. The great lesson is obedience, obedience, obedience. How can we know the voice of the Spirit? It is very easy. How is it easy? There are two powers influencing a man — one draws him toward everything that is good, the other draws him toward everything that is evil. You know who draws you toward evil — the devil. And you know who draws toward that which is good — it is the Holy Spirit. Every good gift comes from Heaven. There is no good in us. Then, henceforth call Him — not "something" but call Him the Spirit of God. If we speak of "something" we shall remain without the Spirit. It will be no good getting thousands to the churches unless we learn the lesson of obedience to the Spirit. If we speak of the Spirit we must obey the Spirit, and from doing that, great results are sure to accrue. If

I had not given up everything to the Spirit, I should not be here today, and I am obliged to say things that make some people regard me almost as insane. But though the whole world sneer at me, I know that I must obey the Spirit.

"QUENCH NOT THE SPIRIT"
Now do not say, "What will people say?" I shall not be here long, but we shall be face to face with God, and we must answer Him. In every prompting of the Spirit, quench it not. God calls and we disobey. "Something" prompts me to pray. "Something" prompts me to give an experience. It is not "something," it is from God. We honour the Father, we honour the Son; when do we honour the Spirit? Who prompts me to call on the Father? It is the Spirit. And who prompts me to call on the Son? It is the Spirit. But who prompts us to pray to the Spirit? Look at our hymnbooks. They praise the Father, and praise the Son, but very few praise the Spirit. Men write hymns that do not praise the Spirit, but I will praise the Spirit of God as long as I live. I shall praise the whole Trinity, and in praising, I shall obey in everything, and the Spirit shall lead me in everything.

I do nothing without having a prayer. It is not enough to hear the voice calling. You must ask, "What time?" and "Where" you are to go. If you are prompted to pray, it is not enough. You must ask to be led to pray again. The great thing is to be led. A lady was prompted to give herself to the Lord, but it was three hours before she was able to make the surrender. She was led, however. Your deep need is direction and guidance in offering yourself. If He says to you "Be silent," be silent. There is no necessity to talk. To be silent may be a way of answering to the call of God. If God calls on you to give out a hymn, or to pray, or to give a testimony, do it. It does not matter if you go into prison or into captivity, if the call comes to you. We were talking about sacrifices. There is nothing worth calling a sacrifice. What have we done for Christ? Someone has never said a word for Christ, and he has been in the Church for years. Say a word for Christ. It is not enough to be there. You must be working there by your word and testimony. If you see a man who cannot say a word for Christ, he does not know what it is. If you find a man who does not say a word for Christ, he has never known Him. The moment you meet Christ you will be on fire; you cannot help speaking. Try to stop the spring and it will burst out at once. If he were silent the stones would talk. You are on fire. The fire is here. You must be baptized with the Spirit of God and fire. It burns everything. If you try to stop the fire, you may get burned yourself.

RESTING UPON GOD

When Abraham obeyed, he was blessed. When Israel went into captivity, God was true to them. When Pharaoh approached, the Israelites were afraid. They saw the enemy, but they did not see God. The Israelites called for God. They asked, "Are there no sepulchres in Egypt that we are brought out?" The nation could see nothing but death. They could not see Canaan and life. God sees life everywhere. If we believe God, we shall see life. We shall lead others to obtain life. The Israelites said, "It would be better for us to serve the Egyptians than to go into the wilderness." Friends, do not obey the enemy any more; obey God. Moses said, "Be not afraid, but stand." "Trust Me," said God. But it is a task to trust when we do not see the future. We want to ask questions even when God invites us to stop and see the heaven of God. Mark this, God shall watch over you. Shall we believe now that God is going to fight for us? That is our danger — to believe that we fight for ourselves, as if God were not with us. We think that God helps us, instead of us helping God. What would you think of a little boy who thinks that it is he who helps his father? God is the great Power, and we are brought in as fellow-workers. Let us rest upon God. The Lord shall fight for us. If we believe, there is nothing that God denies us. Go back to the promises. Go to the last chapter of Matthew again and verse 18. The Lord Jesus Christ, before He ascended to heaven, spoke to His followers and said, "All authority in heaven and earth is given to me." Shall we believe that? "All authority"? If you believe that, the victory shall be with you. Many will try to stand against us. It is better for them to stand aside. The Lord's chariot is going with mighty impetus. John saw the white horse going out. Victory! Woe to anyone who stands before the Lord's chariot! Many will try, but I tell you, "Get aside," for the Lord is in it.

Chapter 11

THE LETTER OF DR. R. A. TORREY, THE RENOWNED REVIVALIST, TO EVAN ROBERTS

32 Loudon Grove,
Princes Park Gate, Liverpool.
November 29, 1904.

Mr Evan Roberts,
Abercynon, Wales
Dear Brother,
I have heard with great joy of the way in which God has been using you as the instrument of His power in different places in Wales. I simply write this letter to let you know of my interest in you, and to tell you that I am praying for you. I have been praying for a long time that God would raise up men of His own choosing in different parts of the world, and mightily anoint them with the Holy Spirit, and bring in a mighty revival of His work. It is so sadly needed in these times.

I cannot tell you the joy that has come to my heart, as I have read of the mighty work of God in Wales. I am praying that God will keep you, simply trusting in Him, and obedient to Him, going not where men shall call you, but going where He shall lead you, and that He may keep you humble, it is so easy for us to become exalted when God uses us as the instruments of His power. It is so easy to think that we are something ourselves, and when we get to thinking that, God will set us aside. May God keep you humble, and fill you more and more with His mighty power.

I hope that some day I may have the privilege of meeting you.
Sincerely Yours,
R. A. Torrey

EVAN ROBERTS' FAVORITE HYMN

Great God of wonders! All Thy ways
Are matchless, Godlike and divine;
But the fair glories of Thy grace
More Godlike and unrivall'd shine:
Who is a pardoning God like Thee?
Or who has grace so rich and free?

In wonder lost, with trembling joy,
We take the pardon of our God,
Pardon for crimes of deepest dye;
A pardon bought with Jesu's blood.
Who is a pardoning God like Thee?
Or who has grace so rich and free?

O may this strange, this matchless grace,
This Godlike miracle of love,
Fill the wide earth with grateful praise,
And all the angelic choirs above:
Who is a pardoning God like Thee?
Or who has grace so rich and free?

Other Christ-exalting and soul-searching titles by
REVIVAL LITERATURE
Healing for the Mind
The Shepherd and His Sheep
Romans Road of Grace
Gospel Missions
Lordship of Christ
Call to the Ministry
Invest for Eternity
Still Waters
Pastures of Tender Grass
Biblical Salvation
Drops from the Honeycombs
Evangelism
Evangelism Without Apology
I Saw the Welsh Revival
Heaven's Throne Gift
The Heavenly Executive
Come O Breath
The Wonder of God's Tomorrow
Reproductions
The Mighty Acts of God in America
Opened Windows
The Phenomena of Pentecost
The Fire of God
Rent Heavens
William Chalmers Burns & Robert Murray McCheyne
Spurgeon, Glorious Spurgeon
Our Beloved Jock
Man in a Hurry
I Must Tell
James Stewart, Missionary
Our Heavenly Inheritance
Daniel Nash: Prevailing Prince of Prayer
Letters from Ruth
Ready for Anything